Senior Real Estate

My Path to Purpose

Dr. Nikki Buckelew, Ph.D.

This book is dedicated to all the Certified Senior Housing Professionals (CSHPs) striving to be "Different" in service to seniors.

Copyright © 2021 Nikki Buckelew

All rights reserved.

ISBN: 978-1-7373129-0-1

CONTENTS

Acknowledgments i

Preface iii

Introduction v

The decision to be different 1

Charting the course 11

Becoming the authority 20

Growth & expansion: Take One 27

Moving on 30

New beginnings 37

Starting over 47

Living my legacy 61

Appendix 65

Let's Connect 73

ACKNOWLEDGMENTS

No doubt this book, nor the story told within its pages, would have been possible without my best friend, husband, business partner and soulmate, Chris. Working with a spouse isn't something just everyone can do. In fact, I often wonder how we do it, but we do and for this I am beyond grateful.

To our kiddos, Kaleb and Dakota: No matter how successful our businesses may become, you two will always be my proudest accomplishments!

A huge thank you to the many coaches and mentors in the real estate industry who encouraged me to follow my heart and passions. First on the list is Gene Lowell Dunlevy who was as much a mom as a real estate broker. Mark Wilkinson, my friend and biggest cheerleader, as well as Art and Anna Kleimer, all whose wise counsel has been replayed in my mind millions of times over the years.

A very special shout out to Julian Codding, my book coach and accountability partner. Without his daily text messages, loving encouragement, and technical direction, this book along with the others in progress would still be hidden somewhere in the archives of my mind.

While this particular story was mine to tell, it's the list of characters with whom I shared the journey thus far that make it the least bit interesting. To you I owe any and all measures of success I may have achieved. To the 1st in Senior Real Estate team, Buckelew Realty

Group and OKC Mature Moves families...You are the true difference makers!

My successes are the result of many partnerships. There are some pretty amazing people out there with whom I get to serve: Jill Huff and her team at Spanish Cove, Julie Davis and her team at Concordia, Caitlin Cairns and her team at Bradford Village, Liz Donnelly, Marie Breshears, Curtis Cain, Jennifer Wright, Steve Cortes, and Marilyn Olson. Thank you for being there even in the hardest of times.

I want to thank Delilah Joiner Martin, program director at Southern Nazarene University, as well as the cadre of professors at SNU. You probably have no idea the impact you have had on my life and career over the years. The time I spent at SNU was pivotal to my exploring the field of aging and ways in which I could become a servant leader.

Finally, I want to acknowledge and thank all the elders in my life who have helped me see that aging is a natural part of living by demonstrating how to do it well. Papa Clinton, Ma Jo, Aunt Sylvia and Uncle Emery, Grandma Kurtz, Mo and Pops, and the many great aunts and uncles on both sides of my family. I know you are all looking down from Heaven and smiling upon us.

Dad...it goes without saying, I left the best for last. You and Mom taught me to love and value people. It's your example and your strength that have equipped me for greatness. I love you!

PREFACE

Over the years I have been asked by individuals and groups both how and why my husband and I made the decision to dedicate our residential real estate practice to serving a more mature clientele. I have told the story so many times that one would think this book would be simple to write. I thought so anyway. It turns out that it isn't as easy as I had hoped. I think it's because I am truly a researcher, teacher and coach at heart and simply telling people how or why I personally did something isn't the same as helping them to do it.

From my perspective, being able to help others forward their personal mission first requires having a true understanding of their motivations, values, skills, resources and goals. That's why I dislike "how-to" books and courses promising a magic formula for success. I prefer personalized business coaching and courses that include critical thinking and experiential learning components.

So, just to be clear, this book is NOT designed to teach people how to build a senior centered real estate niche. We do that at the Seniors Real Estate Institute. This book is just my personal journey to growing a purposeful career serving seniors.

Maybe I should also take this moment to clarify the pronouns I use throughout my writing. While this story is essentially mine, it also involves Chris, my husband of 23 years and business partner of 26. Throughout the book I will speak from my personal perspective and tell my part of the story, so I use the

'I' pronoun. It's more natural, however, for me to refer to 'we' because I can assure you, we have done it all together!

I'm hoping that as you read the book, you will recognize that there is no magic formula and the only requirements for succeeding in service to others (in any discipline) is a true passion for your cause, a willingness to learn (using proven models AND trial and error), some grit, a healthy dab of elbow grease, and as Gary Keller would say, "time on task over time."

If you find our story interesting, but what you are really looking for is a customizable blueprint to follow and a community of servant leaders also committed to serving seniors, you will find that in the courses we offer at the **Seniors Real Estate Institute** (SREI), namely Success in Seniors Real Estate. I discuss how SREI came to be in Chapter 6.

Finally, while this may be obvious, regardless of which path you take, your story and mine will undoubtedly be unique. Even if you choose to grow your own senior centered real estate practice and utilize some of the same proven strategies I use or created, you will put your own special touch on them. Our chapter titles may be similar and a few characters may even overlap, but the plot will take twists and turns. That's what makes life (and the business of serving seniors) interesting.

I can't wait to read your story and I am grateful and humbled that you have chosen to read mine.

INTRODUCTION

This book is long overdue. It started out as a series of blog posts in response to the multitude of requests from agents, probably a lot like you, asking what it takes to create a solid (profitable and purposeful) senior real estate niche. As our businesses evolved over the years, those blog posts became a bit outdated and so I was encouraged by my colleague and book coach, Julian Codding, to turn my articles into a book.

It would probably have been easier to write a book simply outlining the steps for you like we do in our courses at **Seniors Real Estate Institute**, but as a coach I've learned that before anyone can really help someone else be successful at anything, there needs to to be a mutual understanding of what success really means. So, if you don't mind, I want to take a bit of a detour here to further this point.

Success as an outcome is clearly not the same for everyone. I remember when the book by Gary Keller, Dave Jenks, and Jay Papasan came out, *The Millionaire Real Estate Agent*. I knew of agents who dismissed it because they said they didn't really have the desire to be a millionaire. Conversely, I knew others who used the book as their go-to manual for how to make a million dollars year after year!

While one person may simply have gotten licensed to earn enough money to pay their kid's college tuition, another may be driven to amass dozens of rental properties or buy a second home in Italy. Goals are unique to the individual. So, when setting your intention to create a "successful" senior real estate niche, it's critical to define what success really means - to you!

I can tell you that when my husband and I set out to specialize nearly three decades ago, we were very clear about our goals. First and foremost, we wanted to be profitable to the degree that we could afford the things in life we believed would make us feel comfortable. Beyond the typical bills we knew we had to pay, this meant a nice home, reliable cars, vacations, and maybe even a little savings. Setting a goal for a specific level of income to achieve this was a matter of evaluating our expenses, our budget, and the number of transactions necessary to achieve the end result.

Despite what goal setting gurus teach and preach, these types of goals simply didn't motivate me. If you're a servant leader, or you're moving into or beyond middle age, I'm guessing they don't light your fire either. I enjoy making a nice living, but at the end of the day I want more. I want to feel like I'm doing something to contribute to the greater good. I want to make a difference. That said, there's nothing wrong with wanting a more luxurious lifestyle either. My point: To each their own.

Measuring the Unmeasurable

Chances are that you, like me, have been taught that effective goals need to be specific, measurable, achievable, relevant, and time-bound (SMART).

So, how do you set a goal that measures

meaningfulness? How does one evaluate whether their work is fulfilling, purposeful, and aligned with who they really are? Purpose, meaning, and fulfillment are very subjective concepts, so how does one fit them into the SMART goal formula?

You don't. Well, you can, but let's explore a less technical strategy for staying on track.

Business books are generally pretty focused on money, time, and the return on investment for each. What they rarely address, however, is the overall impact of goal achievement on health and wellbeing (even less on relationships).

I could author an entire book on this topic alone, but instead, I'm going to make an assumption about you simply because you have chosen to read this far. I am assuming that you have a servant heart. You may be highly competitive and driven (or not), but either way, you feel the need or desire to direct this inner striving toward a loftier goal.

Permission to set 'feeling' goals.

In her book, *Firestarter Sessions*, Danielle LaPorte discusses how important it is to ask ourselves how we want to feel in addition to what we want to achieve. By first defining how we want to feel, we can then set goals and create strategies designed to help us feel that way.

You hereby have permission to set two types of goals: 1) Quantifiable SMART goals, and 2) Feeling goals.

These are not mutually exclusive. In fact, they should serve to help you focus on achieving your material goals involving money, things, and places, while not letting you lose sight of what is truly most important in life.

The dangers of comparing yourself with others.

This is the last thing I am going to say before diving into what you really came here for.

What's on the following pages is my story. The fact that it's mine means that it's unique to my experience. The only person who gets to determine if any part of it is right or wrong, good or bad, or true or false is me.

As much as I wish you could avoid it, you are going to judge and compare each step of the way. You can't help it. We all do it. It's human. Your limiting beliefs and your ego will both start chattering away. When they do, just remind them that this is not your story and that you'll be writing your own.

Just as my career is and has been a vehicle for achieving my goals, yours should be a vehicle for accomplishing yours. Use my story in whatever way it helps you. You have more potential than you can conceive and if your heart desires, you will likely do far greater things in service for others than I have ever even imagined.

-Nikki

CHAPTER 1: THE DECISION TO BE DIFFERENT

UNREST.
UNCERTAINTY.
TRUTH.
DECISIONS.

My husband and I agreed. We had hit a ceiling. After nearly five years of selling real estate together we were entering our thirties, newly married, and raising a family. Our production was good, but not great. We held our own in the top 20% of agents in our market, but we knew we could do better.

The goal? To grow and expand. Ultimately, to help 100 or more homeowners per year sell their homes. The problem? Me.

Selling real estate no longer excited me. But it was our livelihood and we were making a nice living at it. So now what? Did I just continue selling houses and accept the fact that not everything about making a living is fun. Isn't that what being an adult is all about

- paying the bills?

As an entrepreneur and visionary, my pattern has always been to create, implement, and master a process. Then, when the maintenance phase shows up, I'm out. I've never understood how people could do the exact same job for thirty or more years, much less forty to fifty.

I love love love creation. I enjoy most things about growth and expansion. Maintenance and stability make me crazy.

Another pattern recognizable in my life is that I always seem to be enrolled in some sort of continuing education. I love seminars, college courses, and workshops. Some might say I'm an education junky or perpetual student. I'm okay with that.

Learning is fun for me.

In fact, after I got my master's degree, Chris joked with people saying that his worst nightmare was that eventually I would become, Dr. Nikki Buckelew, REALTOR®. People laughed. I laughed. His nightmare became a reality in 2018 when I finished my doctorate in psychology. I love learning. If you do too and want to geek out by reading my dissertation, let me know! There is a link to it in the appendix.

A slight rewind...

To really understand how the ultimate decision to specialize in the mature market came about, it's important that you know what had been going on in my life behind the scenes during this same time.

While I had picked up a few courses here and there right after high school, I hadn't finished with a degree and that bothered me. So, after Chris and I married and shortly after launching our real estate adventure together, I had gone back to school to check off that particular box. Full time real estate agent. Full time student. Full time mom and wife.

It's amazing how much energy I had when I was in my 20's!

Thank goodness for my husband. Without him picking up the extra workload and kid duty, I could never have done it.

When enrolling, I really didn't care too much about what degree I would get, I simply just wanted to parlay my previous college credits into something that would result in a certificate on my wall.

In my research, I found a nearby accredited university offering what is referred to as a degree completion program for adult students. It involved a four hour class one evening a week and was extremely writing intensive - right up my alley! The degree? A bachelor of science in Family Studies and Gerontology. It would take 18 months. I was all in - sign me up.

It was as if all the stars aligned and I was unknowingly being equipped for the job I was made to do.

As fate would have it, as I grappled with whether or

not selling real estate would be my life's work, my university introduced a new graduate degree program offered in the same format in which I had just completed my undergrad degree. Earning a master's degree in counseling psychology would require yet another two years of school. Completing it would qualify me to take the state exam for Licensed Professional Counselor (LPC) and give me the credentials to do what I really wanted to do - help people. Diving off into the proverbial deep end, I signed up for another student loan and back to school I went. Two years later I had earned a graduate degree and yes, I was still selling real estate. Successfully, I might add.

Gifts from the Universe

Has there ever been a time when you knew you wanted something different, but didn't know what that something was?

All I knew at this point is that I had a strong desire to help people. In fact, it was the part of selling houses I enjoyed most. Unfortunately, the daily grind that was cold calling, open house sitting, and driving buyers all over town was exhausting. Industry award ceremonies had become all about who made the most money or closed the most transactions. I was growing tired of the "more is better" mantra and the world domination mindset.

Wasn't there more to life? Shouldn't my career serve as more than just a vehicle for getting my bills paid?

You may be wondering by this point if I am ever

going to actually tell you how we made the decision to specialize in helping seniors. If you're willing to stick with me for just a bit longer, I promise it will all come together. Or, you could simply skip over to Chapter 2 and start there!

Everything we do is part of a greater story unfolding.

As I continued to search for what would be next, life delivered to us a couple of very unexpected yet amazing gifts. The first gift was personal. To date I'm not sure it has anything at all to do with my career or real estate decisions, but it certainly changed the way I look at life. This gift helped me to recognize there are no coincidences.

Gift #1: Dakota Annabelle

Still in a state of career decision making limbo, but certain I wanted to positively impact the lives of others, I elected to sit for the state LPC exam. And while I was at it, why not go ahead and get certified as an alcohol and drug counselor (CADC) as well. Upon passing the two state exams, I was now required to complete 3000 hours of counseling under a supervising LPC.

Sidenote: *I firmly believe newly licensed real estate agents should have to undergo an equally rigorous process before unleashing them to handle the most valuable asset most people possess.*

Still serving as the rainmaker for our real estate team, I played real estate agent by day and counselor by night and on weekends. Chris continued to juggle the other aspects of our business.

While not glamorous, the best way for me to log my required counseling hours was to contract with various agencies who served low-income families. When I wasn't visiting subsidized housing complexes, longterm care facilities, and places where having a concealed carry came in handy, I contracted as a therapist and case worker at adolescent mental health facilities, senior diagnostic centers, and clinics offering DUI courses and assessments.

Keep in mind what I said earlier about my preference for starting, learning, and mastering things. This new adventure was interesting and challenging for a while, but then reality set in. Despite my efforts to make a positive difference in the lives of the clients I served, the bureaucratic red tape and questionable business practices were beginning to infringe on my values of integrity and honesty. These value conflicts resulted in more than a few nights of lost sleep.

Nonetheless, I'm certainly glad I stuck it out just a little longer. Just as I finalized the required supervision, something beautiful occurred. I received a phone call from a foster parent of a young girl I had been counseling. The child was going to be placed for adoption and she wanted to know if my husband and I had any interest in adopting her.

I believe nothing happens by accident and there are no coincidences in life.

After a lengthy but worthwhile process, we welcomed this beautiful 9-year-old girl into our home as our daughter. It turned out that the path I had been following wasn't a career path at all. Instead it was leading us to the greatest gift ever.

Now our little girl is all grown up with a family of her own. She's married and the mother of our three perfect grandchildren who affectionately call us Oompah and Nini.

Gift #2: A Wise Old Woman named Ms. Sanders

As if the first gift wasn't quite enough, the Universe delivered yet again. This gift, however, instead of coming in the form of a young girl, came in the form of an elderly woman. More specifically, a beautiful petite Octogenarian. She was about 4 feet 7 inches tall with fiery red hair and pale white skin. She sat with tears streaming down her face. I sat beside her and began to inquire as to the source of her tears.

My job was to assess her situation, give a diagnosis, and develop a treatment plan.

As her new therapist, I wanted to understand her and empathize. Ms. Sanders, like many of the new residents, wasn't thrilled about her new accommodations. She commented that she felt alone, abandoned, and scared. I asked a few clarifying questions, but before I could complete the field in her chart with the diagnosis of depression, Ms. Sanders abruptly sat upright. She looked at me square in the eyes and firmly stated, "I'm not depressed, I'm angry."

Well, I said, "Tell me more about your anger." As it turned out, her daughter had finalized the sale of her nearby home and then arranged for the liquidation of her remaining personal belongings. Ms. Sanders further pinpointed the source of her anger by exclaiming, "My daughter gave away my refrigerator. She did it without even asking me. She just gave it away." Tears continued to stream down her cheeks.

I learned that her daughter had negotiated the refrigerator as a part of the sale and had apparently done so without consulting her mother. As an experienced real estate agent, I knew this to be common practice, so I attempted to normalize her daughter's decision by explaining that buyers often ask for appliances to remain in the home as a part of the overall negotiation. This naive attempt to make things better was met with a great deal of hostility. Whether this was common practice or not was no consolation for Ms. Sanders. "It was my house. My refrigerator. She had no right," she continued.

It was in fact her refrigerator, her house, and her decisions to make — yet she wasn't consulted. To Ms. Sanders it seemed as if a cadre of real estate agents, her daughter, and the purchasers had all colluded to deprive her of her beloved harvest gold double door refrigerator. I'm not sure if they did or didn't, but at the very least she had been deprived of decisions that were rightfully hers to make.

Sidenote: *Anyone working with older adults should pick up the book by David Solie, "How to Say it to Seniors: Closing* *the Communication Gap with Our Elders," for more on returning control to his or her rightful owner.*

Over the course of the next hour, Ms. Sanders, whose short term memory was questionable, but longterm memory vivid, shared a heartwarming story surrounding the purchase of the refrigerator in question. She recounted with relative precision the appliance store where it had been purchased. She remembered the price her late husband had negotiated and a number of other details involving its acquisition. The refrigerator was the couple's first new appliance and the year was 1968.

To say that I was moved would be an understatement. I was also compelled. Compelled to help the Ms. Sanders of the world, along with their sons and daughters. Help with what, you might ask? Help them to better navigate such complex and emotionally charged transitions so that, in the end, the family system remains intact and the older adult still has his or her dignity.

Clarity is Power

The clarity of that moment is vivid. It was as if a switch was flipped inside me.

Ms. Sanders' story had a profound impact on me that day. It was like the real estate agent, the daughter, the granddaughter, and the therapist inside me collided, spawning new insight and purpose. I knew with absolute clarity what my next vocational chapter would be.

People in ministry often refer to being "called" to serve. While I have never really heard or felt such a calling myself, I imagine this to be a similar experience. It was a defining moment. A certainty. A sense of purpose unlike any I had ever felt before.

It occurred to me... I could be both. I could literally do both. As a real estate agent, I could also be a therapist. In fact, most real estate agents will tell you that when they're helping home sellers or buyers, especially during times of crises (i.e. job loss, divorce, foreclosure, probate, etc.), they sometimes feel like they need a psychology degree.

I went home that day and proclaimed to Chris that, not only was I planning to stay in the real estate business, we were going to specialize in serving seniors. With a dazed and confused look, he asked me if I was sure (or maybe he asked if I had lost my mind - it's hard to remember that far back). I told him I had never been so sure in my entire life.

Now it was simply a matter of charting the course.

CHAPTER 2: CHARTING THE COURSE

THE SEARCH FOR A PROVEN MODEL

The decision was official that we would begin focusing our full attention on serving the senior market. Not only did it make solid business sense (very important to my husband and business partner), it fulfilled my inner drive to be of service to others.

Yes, I know that real estate agents help people every day and that you don't have to serve seniors to be a servant leader. I have plenty of colleagues who are satisfied to help buyers and sellers in the traditional sense and who feel completely fulfilled doing so. It simply didn't fulfill me.

As a result of our years of training with Keller Williams Realty, and more specifically the lessons from *The Millionaire Real Estate Agent* book, we knew enough to seek out a proven model to follow. This would shorten our learning curve and help us in avoiding pitfalls and mistakes along the way.

My initial research led me to the then newly available Senior Real Estate Specialist (SRES) designation. This was some time before NAR was involved and the organization was still in its relative infancy. Tim Corliss, the founder of the group offering the course, had put the courses and designation together in an effort to help agents better serve the older adult market.

Although I had earned advanced degrees, I knew there had to be more to learn, especially related to seniors and real estate. I was right, however, I wasn't necessarily pleased with everything I would learn. The nearest class at the time (pre-online learning) was a few hours away by car in Dallas, Texas. I put the registration on my credit card and headed south.

Upon arrival, I was surprised the class size was so small - only about 8 people. The instructor was enthusiastic, although he clearly didn't know much about the South or about Texas. Being from New England, his attempts at humor didn't always land quite right. Nonetheless, we made it through the two day training without incident.

While I picked up a few helpful tidbits of information, much of what was taught could just as easily have been read from a textbook. The curriculum lacked the one thing I was looking for - a business model. I was seeking a blueprint that would guide me through the steps of creating a successful niche working with senior adults. In all actuality, what

I gained was even more valuable.

What I observed during the two days was that most real estate agents in the class didn't get it. They were there to earn letters to list on their business cards somehow indicating they knew what they were doing - even if they didn't. A few even stated directly that they saw the age wave coming and were simply there to learn how to add more deals to their bottom lines.

It also seemed to be the wild wild west as far as creating a senior centered niche was concerned. Even the instructor, the appointed expert in the room, didn't have the answers. At one point he even had the audacity to say that if we were lucky, some senior without a family may even put us in their will if we do a good job for them. The class laughed. I was disgusted.

It was that weekend when I knew - without one ounce of doubt or reservation - that we would master the art of serving seniors and that it was up to me to create a model that worked. A model uniquely designed to help me (and people like me) accomplish a mission - to serve senior homeowners in a way that empowered and equipped them to make informed real estate and senior living decisions.

Mastering the 55+ Housing Market

Among the first steps in my newly formed strategy for mastering the 55+ housing market, I went into overdrive attempting to learn as much as I could about all things senior living. Within a couple of months I had catalogued every housing development, subdivision, senior living community, Continuing Care Retirement Community (CCRC) and assisted living in our service area.

I toured almost all of them personally and got to know the marketing directors, sales reps, and anyone else who would talk with me. During the course of my tours I asked a million questions. I wanted to learn about the obstacles incoming residents faced, the challenges associated with new move-in's, and the means by which they attracted prospects to their communities.

Some of the marketing directors were welcoming and cordial, while others were distant and cool. It didn't take long to recognize that being a real estate agent wasn't working in my favor. I had a number of unreturned phone calls, a few polite "no thank you's" and a variety of simple dismissals. Nonetheless, I didn't let that distract me from my goal. It was important that I understood all the options available to senior clients, and so I focused on the communities and staff members who were willing to give me a chance.

My first referral came not long after calling on a senior housing complex catering to low-income individuals. I eagerly went to meet Kate at her home. She reminded me a lot of Ms. Sanders with her petite build and somewhat sad affect. Her home was modest and clean, but it seemed as though something were missing. Kate shared with me that her brother and lifelong roommate had recently passed away. He had looked after her most of their adult lives. Suffering from debilitating epilepsy, Kate never married and was unable to drive. Now, with him gone, she was a bit lost and quite lonely.

When I asked her what she looked forward to most about moving into a retirement community, Kate said she looked forward to not eating alone.

As I learned more about the various types of communities and levels of care, it became clear to me that not only would I need to know about the buildings and the services offered there, but I would need to establish relationships with the directors of marketing. It seemed to me at the time (and I would be right) they were in the most likely position to build relationships with potential residents and to refer to people like me.

More importantly, however, I needed to know more about the clients themselves. What did they need? What were their biggest fears and challenges? How could I be of service?

Getting to Know Senior Homeowners

Learning about senior living communities was a simple task compared to getting to know senior homeowners. It's not like they had big signs out front that said, "Seniors live here." I needed to have more conversations with people like Ms. Sanders.

Thankfully, we had developed a number of solid relationships over the years and so we called upon our colleagues and friends to help us out. Letters and phone calls (yes, actual phone calls) went out first to past clients, friends, family, and neighbors informing them of our intentions to specialize in serving seniors and their families.

The calls and responses from our letters were surprisingly encouraging. People told us how much they wished they had known what we were doing back when they had to help an older family member with a transition. I gained great invaluable insights from each of these conversations. Insights which would later serve to inform our various service offerings and help us construct our value propositions.

I also reached out to the marketing directors I had become acquainted with at several of the independent and assisted living communities. They collaborated with me to coordinate focus groups made up of their residents. Who better to learn from than those who had already been through the process of relocation?

The focus groups were invaluable! Participants gave us huge insight into the obstacles they faced as they began to consider downsizing. They were also more than happy to tell us about all the mistakes they had made, as well as the top service providers they used to accomplish their moves and subsequent home sales. Some participants had not yet moved and were eager to tell us about their fears, concerns, and perceived obstacles.

Taking time to learn from professionals, senior adults, and caregivers was worth every minute. I gained so much value from this series of exercises I was able to craft a very specific strategy for making sure that our mature clients got exactly what they needed for a successful relocation and home sale experience.

Getting the Word Out

Creating a unique senior-centered service offering was one thing, but effectively articulating it to the masses was yet another. We knew the traditional residential real estate marketing and advertising methods quite well. Using magazine ads, newspaper classifieds, flyers, open houses, and email marketing was commonplace in real estate at this time. The internet was not yet the end all be all solution at this point, so no such thing as social media or Google. We were just happy our MLS was online!

We needed a new approach. We needed to be different. This new strategy focused on a demographic rather than geographic farm - new terrain. We set out to chart the territory and create our own map.

As I mentioned earlier, senior living community market directors were already a bit skeptical of us. Real estate agents tend to rate up there with used car salespeople and trial attorneys (no offense to either) when it comes to reputation. Sadly, a few bad apples spoil the bunch, as they say.

Knowing the highest and best use of our time wasn't designing marketing materials or creating flyers and websites, we invested in outside help from a local marketing and public relations firm. The two owners had done work for us previously and had recently launched their own firm. We knew they were talented, and as a startup they were also hungry for business.

It took a series of meetings for them to really understand what we were doing. Let's face it, I'm not sure we even knew what we were doing yet! It was all still theory. During our meetings, I was nothing if not passionate. I remember getting so excited one day that Brad, the design guy, burst into laughter saying, "I hope all our clients will be this enthusiastic about what they do!"

The interview process ultimately helped us to gain clarity about what we were really trying to do and the value we had to offer. With blind trust and a checkbook in hand, we turned our marketing and branding over to them. They knocked it out of the park, but not without some major push back from us initially.

The first recommendation came instructing us to plaster the tagline "1st in Senior Real Estate" on every piece of marketing we had. All of it. We were skeptical to say the least. Terrified too. What if it didn't work? What if non-seniors wouldn't do business with us? What if we were breaking fair-housing laws?

What if. What if? What if?

But then it worked.

We were not only fortunate enough to be the first in our market to cater exclusively to the 55+ consumer, but our approach was completely unique. We were offering seniors (and any age homeowner who wanted it) a soup to nuts experience including consulting, moving, estate liquidation support, and residential real estate sales.

Our services were both personal and hands-on. Our brand proudly boasted **"1st in Senior Real Estate"** and we meant it.

CHAPTER 3: BECOMING THE AUTHORITY

EDUCATE.
EMPOWER.
EQUIP.

At the same time we were learning how to better serve mature homeowners, we were also educating and teaching. I knew from my days as a therapist that in order to be recognized as an authority in the aging services space we had to drastically differentiate ourselves from the typical real estate crowd. Real estate agents aren't generally well-received by those advocating for seniors. In fact, people in most types of sales are often perceived as predators, simply looking to make a sale. Unless you understand the plight of the aging services community of advocates and can speak their language, you may as well be in a foreign country.

Partnering with senior living communities

It was one thing visiting senior living communities

with a goal of learning about them and their services. Getting them to take time to learn about us and what we had to offer was a whole different story. While I knew we were different than typical agents, they hadn't gotten the memo.

Community representatives, poised as gatekeepers and tasked with protecting their residents, referred only to reputable vendors (and friends) who had passed their various litmus tests. It was clear I would have to earn their respect and prove myself worthy of their trust.

"Fair enough," I said to myself. "I can appreciate their positions and am willing to do what it takes to prove my value and trustworthiness."

I am a follower of Zig Ziglar who said, "You can have everything in life you want, if you just help enough other people get what they want." With this in mind, I set out to find out what these communities wanted. Not just the community, but the person who represented the community. These were real people, just like me. They were doing a job, but also had lives, families, and goals.

It turns out their goals and needs weren't much different than my own. They needed more leads (move-ins), more time (fewer hassles), and more support (team members). They had occupancy quotas, limited budgets, and were at the mercy of their corporate offices or boards of directors. But most of all, they wanted to be of service to seniors - just like me.

As I found more ways to help them achieve their goals, they began to answer the phone when I called. I found myself not only marketing homes for sale, but senior living community apartments as well. It was my goal to help them find new residents because new residents for them meant new clients for me too.

Looking back on this endeavor, there are at least three valuable lessons I learned in my attempts to partner with communities. We not only spend a lot of time on these in our SREI courses, but they are lessons I remind myself about each day in my own businesses:

1. Give before you receive - come from contribution.

2. Relationships are critical - rapport building takes time, effort, and consistency.

3. Focus on quality over quantity - not everyone is a values match.

Developing a strong resource team

I have never really liked networking. Some people love it and have made a nice living using professional networking as their strategy. I am more about education, and for me, going to meetings just for the sake of exchanging business cards has never been appealing. That said, I knew that it was going to be important to not only get the word out about what we do and the differences between us and other real estate teams, I needed to know what resources were out there.

There were two or three networking groups in our

market which were primarily made up of aging services professionals. This meant a fairly significant contingent of marketers in the healthcare space such as home health, private duty care, hospice, behavioral health, and durable medical equipment. Then there were those who worked in insurance, finance, and legal disciplines. Of course there were also a number of people from not-for-profit agencies and a few senior living communities. No real estate agents to speak of.

One particular group hosted a special guest speaker each month and this was appealing to me. In fact, it is how I met my first estate liquidator. I approached her following her presentation and requested a meeting over coffee. Much to my surprise, she agreed. This would be the beginning of a beautiful and mutually beneficial long term relationship. She referred to us regularly and we were able to refer to her often as well.

While I met a few other people at these meetings, I ultimately found that the marketers changed jobs so often it made my head spin. One week they would be with a home care company and the next peddling behavioral health for a local hospital. I kept going until I found a core group of professionals with whom my values aligned and our respective fields seemed to make logical sense when it came to supporting one another and our mutual clients.

After attending meetings, I connected with specific people and scheduled time to get to know them. My goal was to find out what they did and whether or not my particular expertise and service offering would benefit them or those they served.

Educating, equipping, empowering

Thankfully, I am blessed with the gift of gab. Unlike many who would rather die than have to stand in front of a room and talk, I LOVE public speaking and teaching. As an agent leader in real estate offices, I am often called upon to teach. It has always come naturally to me. As Danielle LaPorte would say, it's my zone of genius.

With this in mind, it just made sense to me at the time to put together a series of talks on the topic of downsizing. Offering classes geared toward mature longtime homeowners who might be struggling with the idea of or tasks associated with relocation, I first offered myself up to senior living communities. It was a way I could provide something of mutual value, while also creating an excuse for them to reach out to their prospect list.

Later, we marketed the talks to local not-for-profits and civic groups. It wasn't long before I was teaching or speaking at least once a week and had developed my own presentation titled Downsizing Made Easy: 5 Easy Steps to a Successful Move. Instead of me always having to look for places to go, groups started calling me. Each time I spoke I had at least one person come up afterward to share their personal story and say "thanks for doing what you do."

For more information on the Downsizing Made Easy Presentation System, go to www.seniorsrealestateinstitute.com/DSME.

Teaching is personally gratifying and fills my soul.

Some who shared their stories also remarked how they regretted not having had the information many years earlier when helping their own families. This compelled me to spread the word even more quickly and with more intention.

Giving these talks and showing people that I not only had a deep desire to serve, but that I also had the tools, resources, and ability to simplify the process for people having lived in their homes virtually forever, provided me the credibility and validity I needed in order to earn the respect and trust of those in the aging services community.

I'll talk more about how our seminars have evolved over the years in Chapter 7.

Thinking outside the box

As I have said, we first launched our marketing campaign by reaching out to the people we knew and focusing on the relationships we already had (i.e. past clients, family, friends, and professional alliances). Next, we partnered with select senior living communities and we conducted seminars and educational talks anywhere people gathered.

We embraced our new brand and perfecting our value proposition with every client we served. Things were going well, but nothing ever moves fast enough for me - just ask my husband.

With no model to follow, we were building the proverbial airplane in the air.

At this stage in our career, the internet wasn't nearly as robust as it is now and frankly, data was limited. We lived in a neighborhood that seemed to have a lot of retirees and so we started there and expanded to similar neighborhoods over time. Trying everything from door knocking and door hangers to mailers and cold calling, it was clear that our message was not getting through.

We needed leverage.

Of course I don't do anything half-way, so in order to meet all the people in our neighborhood and share with them the solutions we had for helping mature homeowners, I needed a way to get them all together. Naturally, it made sense to simply organize a neighborhood association. This was then followed by a home watch program. At this point I am pretty sure there was little doubt in Chris's mind that I had gone off my rocker. He may have been right.

Our first meeting was made up of a group of hand selected people who had been strategically chosen to put things in motion. Our real estate team sponsored the venue, flyers, newsletters, and signs. It was a hit. Not only did we get to meet a large percentage of the residents, but we forged relationships with key "watchdogs" who kept us in the loop about literally EVERYTHING.

If I'm being completely honest, I'm not sure I would do that again at this stage in my life. At that stage, however, it was the bomb (in a good way). The internet and social media groups of today make it much simpler to engage with existing neighborhood associations and become established as the authority.

The key: Personal connections - not traditional advertising.

Agent referrals

Another out-of-the-box strategy for generating leads happened mostly by accident. Our brand was becoming more well known in local real estate circles. Agents within and outside our brokerage started calling us for advice about senior clients. In some cases they had already listed the property and weren't sure how to deal with someone who wouldn't leave for showings or who had a very outdated or cluttered home.

Some just wanted advice, guidance, and resources, but most of them just wanted to pass the client on to our team for an agreed upon referral fee. We were happy to help. It was a win for the client, a win for us, and a win for any agent who found they were outside their scope of expertise.

Once we realized that many agents simply ignored these clients in their day to day practice of lead generation, we began putting the word out that we could help. It didn't take long before we found agents in our own office regularly referring clients to us they had connected with through cold-calling or door-knocking. This was especially true if agents perceived the sales cycle to be longer than normal.

Throwing spaghetti is messy.

I like to say that I enjoy throwing spaghetti on the wall and seeing what sticks. Whatever sticks is what we keep doing and whatever falls to the floor we simply sweep up and put it in the trash. Believe me when I say that I have thrown lots of spaghetti to date. It's messy. But so is growing a business. Sometimes I throw the same spaghetti more than once just to see what happens.

What's with the pasta metaphor?

Part of my story of success includes a number of failed attempts. We have tried many marketing strategies over the years and some things simply didn't work. Here are just a few...

Direct mail postcards. We've spent hundreds of dollars (Chris says more like thousands) over the years with not much to show for it. I have determined in my anecdotal research that older adults receive so much junk mail, mostly in the form of postcards, they simply don't read it. When they do read it, they are skeptical. Some just flatly resent getting them.

Magazine ads. Again, thousands of dollars wasted on this particular marketing strategy. That said, we have gotten occasional positive results from select publications when marketing our seminars.

Health fairs and expos. I have set up, torn down, and sat for hours at more of these than I can count over the years. What I can count on one hand, however, is how many transactions have resulted from such time wasters. I did find that attending them as a spectator and researching the key players in the industry was helpful in the early years when growing my resource list.

Social media paid advertising. When social media became the best thing in real estate since the MLS, we tried. And then we tried again. Oh, and one more time, just for good measure. My experience is that our audience (mostly older seniors versus baby boomers) is not engaging online for our services. Yes, they follow their grandkids, classmates, and cute puppies and such, but they don't select a real estate agent from a Facebook ad.

Sidenote: *I'm guessing that over time social media and online marketing will become much more important in connecting with the older adult market. The current generation of older seniors (80 and beyond) just don't use it much, while the boomers are far more open to engaging online. As they reach their later years, I'm really hoping for a higher adoption rate of electronic signing too!*

CHAPTER 4: GROWTH AND EXPANSION: TAKE ONE

SERVING SENIORS TAKES A VILLAGE

Building a business isn't always easy and if anyone thinks otherwise, they have never really done it. There are always new things to learn, hurdles to jump, and obstacles to overcome. One of the biggest hurdles for us was staffing. As we grew in production we became even more committed to delivering a high level of value to our clients and to do that, we needed more hands on deck.

Key Hire #1: Administrative support

I am fortunate enough to be married to someone who understands and is proficient at the operational side of owning and running a business. That said, Chris isn't what I would call an 'attention to detail' guy. He is more of a 'done is better than perfect' guy. So once we were up and running, our little team of two required someone who could focus on crossing T's and dotting I's.

We started out with a part time person. Then another. Then another. This position was tough to fill and was even harder to train. Nonetheless, necessary. Finally, we located a full time person who was able to keep up with us and she stayed on board for a few years. I have resolved this to be the nature of business going forward.

When things got busier, we also hired a part-time runner. Darrel, a retired civil engineer, worked 2-3 days a week in the morning. He delivered pre-listing materials, planted and retrieved yard signs, changed out sign riders, and ran other errands as needed. Darrel gave great hugs too!

Looking back over the years, we have had a number of administrative people. Some have been talented and others, not so much. It's definitely a key position and not an easy one to fill. More on this in chapter 7 when I talk about staffing and the re-launch.

Key Hire #2: Move Manager

With more and more clients downsizing into senior living communities, we quickly realized there were a lot of extra details we had to manage. This was especially true when homeowners had lived in the same home for several decades, had little or no local family support, or had physical or cognitive impairments.

To fulfill our value proposition of facilitating hassle-free turnkey relocations, we found ourselves working overtime. We rolled up our sleeves and helped clients with everything. This included space planning, packing, unpacking, resettling, coordinating, estate sales and more. Although I loved this hands on approach, Chris and I just didn't have the skillset or the time to do it for everyone we served. Especially if we were going to grow and expand.

According to my husband and close friends, "I couldn't take all of them to raise."

Having launched our original senior centered real estate practice in the early 2000's, the move management industry was barely in its infancy. As I looked for people who had the title of move manager from coast to coast, the only ones I could find were in Indiana, Ohio, and California. Being in Oklahoma, this did me little good.

Our only option at this point was to hire and train our own move manager. Asking around for recommendations, I was introduced to a young woman who had recently completed a masters degree in gerontology from a nearby state university. Her name was Shaunda.

In many ways she was overqualified and could easily have found work that paid more than we could ever have matched. But Shaunda didn't want to work for a government agency where she punched a clock and sat behind a desk. She wanted to make a real difference and provide direct service to clients who needed a helping hand. Hiring her was a no brainer.

Shaunda took a risk and so did we because neither of us had any idea what we were doing. We simply knew that we wanted to serve seniors and so we made a commitment to figure it out together. It didn't take long before she was handling all the move-related details herself. When we didn't have a move on the schedule, Shaunda spent time forging new partnerships with senior communities and nurturing relationships with existing ones. She also attended networking functions and vetted vendors who were now clambering to be a part of our resource team.

Shaunda spoke the language of aging services providers. Clients loved her, communities adored her, and we couldn't have done it without her!

My rule is that if you don't have a move manager - you are one.

Over the years we have hired our share of move managers and other relocation-related support staff. We have also contracted with outside move managers - some have been better than others. Because this is such an integral position for our team, my preference has been to keep it in-house allowing for continuity of service and quality control.

For more information on adding a move management division to an existing real estate practice, visit seniorsrealestateinstitute.com/managing-mature-moves.

Key Hire #3: Business coaches

While we had become fairly successful as real estate

salespeople and were gradually becoming highly efficient and effective at serving mature homeowners, we knew we needed to become better business people.

It was time to start running our business like a business.

Despite the fact we were now closing around 75 transactions annually, we didn't really have standards, systems, or anything resembling an employee handbook or standard operating procedures. Our leadership skills were lacking and we were each working 60-80 hours a week.

Of the plethora of well known coaches and trainers specializing in real estate business planning, marketing, and operations, none seemed to have a clue how to coach us on running a senior centered business. They wanted to tell us how we could better 'sell' to seniors, but they didn't grasp the concept that we had developed a complete turnkey relocation process. Moreover, the fact that we actually cared about our clientele beyond the real estate sales transaction was a foreign concept to most of them.

We needed business coaches who thought beyond the traditional real estate model.

Then we met Art and Anna. They were seasoned business coaches who had also owned and operated a highly successful real estate team. More importantly, however, they "got us" and were as excited as we were about the niche we had created. They understood our vision and recognized that we had the potential to do great things. My guess is this had a lot to do with the fact they had both helped aging parents or other family members and understood the challenges associated with what we did.

Writing that first check was a big step. We were going to be paying more for coaching than we paid for our mortgage every month! As it turned out, this was one of the best decisions of our careers. After just one year of working weekly with our coaches, our small team achieved our sales goal of over 100 transactions for the year.

We were no longer working evenings and weekends. We got our financials in order. We had a solid business plan. We were working smarter not harder.

By now, our small team was highly profitable and our senior clients were getting a level of service unmatched by any other team or single agent in our market. Referrals kept pouring in and we found ourselves once again ready for expansion.

Key Hire #4: Buyer agents

Looking back on it now, I am pretty sure we already knew we needed to bring on agents solely focused on converting and contracting homebuyer leads. The fact is, we were simply unsure of how to go about it.

Our coaches helped us clarify our expectations about what these team members would do, as well as how our team would support and train them. Considering we had an inventory of anywhere from 15 to 20 listings at any given time, it was important to us that we had top quality people to field incoming leads and convert them into exclusive buyer agreements.

Sidenote: *We had a team standard to only work with home buyers who would sign an exclusive contract with us.*

Training new team members on how to effectively present our value proposition to prospective buyers was key. Once they got it, our buyer specialists were highly productive and profitable. That said, we were still learning how to be leaders. So, naturally we went through a few talented people before we figured out how to hang on to the good ones and let the others go.

Having buyer agents in place and an administrative team to keep things on track, Chris and I were able to reduce our weekend and evening hours, focusing more on leadership, expansion, and oversight.

CHAPTER 5: MOVING ON

THE NEXT ADVENTURE

Before we even realized it (about 5 years), we had built a real estate practice centered on the mature market that had actual equity. This was unheard of in the industry at that time, as most people simply walked away from their businesses when they decided to stop selling.

We were now ready for the next adventure.

Tired of the Oklahoma winters and desperate for a change of scenery (one where the water was blue), we set our sights on a cross country relocation. This meant making some decisions. We could either start a new sales team in another market, go into brokerage management, or get out of the real estate space altogether. We chose door number two - brokerage management.

Our own office manager, Gene, otherwise known in

our company as a 'team leader,' had been telling me that I should become a team leader myself. Gene assured me that I was capable and that it could also be a way for us to earn some ownership shares if successful. That was somewhat appealing, but not as appealing as the idea of relocating to another state. More specifically, Florida.

The challenge? We had no idea how to sell what we had built.

This was yet another pivotal time in our careers when our business coaches proved invaluable. We had no idea how much our real estate business was worth nor how to market it for sale. If it hadn't been for Art and Anna, we could have easily left thousands of dollars on the table. In fact, we probably would have simply closed up shop and headed to the coast.

With the help of our coaches and after careful evaluation and consultation, we were able to determine the value of our current listing inventory, the probability or likelihood of repeat clients, the estimated longterm revenue from our senior centered marketing program, and the projected impact of our brand over time.

With that, we created an "offer to sell." And it did - in a week. Sunny Florida, here we come! Onward to our next adventure.

And the next.

And the next.

CHAPTER 6: NEW BEGINNINGS

REPURPOSING SAWDUST

When Chris and I packed up and said goodbye to our Oklahoma home and businesses, we thought we were saying goodbye forever to senior real estate sales as well. In fact, we left virtually everything behind for the new owners because it never really occurred to us that we would need or want it again.

We spent one year in Florida, followed by one year in Louisiana, as managers of real estate offices. During that time, our primary job descriptions included recruiting, training, and leading (both new and seasoned real estate agents), as well as providing operational support to the owners. It didn't take long for me to recognize that this was NOT my zone of genius. Chris agreed.

We loved the warm weather and being near the Gulf, but decided to pursue new opportunities unrelated to brokerage management.

The next stop on our journey was Austin, Texas, headquarters for Keller Williams Realty International. Gifted with the ability to deal with high maintenance and high powered women (working together in close quarters), Chris was offered a corporate position in the coaching division. He worked alongside the Keller Williams executive team as an operations manager. Having gained recent experience managing offices, he also served as a coach to market center administrators around the country.

As for me, I concluded (along with a number of former supervisors) that I wasn't cut out for being an employee. Instead, it made more sense for me to do what I knew I was good at - real estate sales. I got my Texas real estate license and went about establishing myself as a senior real estate expert in the Austin market.

Around the same time I got my first listing appointment, I also got a phone call from the President of the Keller Williams Realty coaching department. I was offered an opportunity to be involved with a new program being developed. This new initiative called BOLD would afford me the ability to travel around the country coaching, training, teaching, and selling. It was perfect!

Handing off my new client (a senior home seller) and newly acquired listing to a colleague, I abandoned my newly launched real estate sales business and embarked on a two year "BOLD" adventure.

One thing I observed as I traveled from city to city presenting BOLD was that while the overall program itself was excellent and contained many positives, it was rather prescriptive. In other words, instead of helping agents discover what worked for them, it mandated a set of "proven" sales tactics without regard for personality, behavioral style, or personal preference (a.k.a. zone of genius). Agents who were already assertive and who easily embraced a more transactional style of operating did quite well, however, those who preferred a more relational approach found the methods off-putting and abrasive.

In fact, I found that I was attempting to teach and coach others to use methods that I personally never preferred in my own business practices. I had, of course, tried them all because it's what agents were taught as fundamentals to being in real estate sales.

Another issue I grappled with was that the measurement of BOLD success was purely quantitative. It was all about how many sales, listings, referrals, and closings an agent could accumulate during the 8-week program. Despite the assertion the program was designed to help agents create "a life by design," the predominant emphasis was on numbers, lacking any qualitative measurement such as personal, relational, or vocational satisfaction.

Knowing how important it had been to me that my real estate practice feed my soul, I shared with select agents along the way how creating a niche had helped me to find a renewed passion for real estate.

I encouraged disillusioned participants to seek out their own niche, whether the mature audience or some other specialty, and to utilize the tools taught in the program toward that end. Many took my advice and were able to successfully finish the program. As I began teaching others the benefits of niche marketing, I realized that it was a piece of the puzzle that more people needed to hear. Nonetheless, I was far too busy and involved in my current project to do anything about it just yet. On a back burner it went.

Then one day I received a phone call from an agent in Orlando, Florida. Michele was calling me on the recommendation from her team leader who knew of my former success in the senior real estate space. She was looking for a proven model. Heart centered, faith based, and eager to serve, I knew instantly that Michele was a perfect fit for this highly specialized niche. I told her I would put together whatever I could find and get it to her.

As happenstance would have it, not long after our initial conversation, I was scheduled to present a program in Orlando. I dug out piles of old documents, handouts, flyers, and publications I thought might prove useful to Michele. This was before it was easy to share documents online and much of what I had created was done on Microsoft Publisher. If you are 50 or older you may remember this pre-Canva graphic design and presentation program. Ugh.

There were no outlines, no guides, and no workbooks...just a stack of stuff.

I left the stack on her desk with a sticky note saying, "Good luck." With random materials at her fingertips, Michele would call me on occasion and we would talk through how I had used certain strategies and tools. Essentially, I was trying to convey the method behind my madness. Michele was always excited and enthusiastic (I would go so far as to say passionate) and she definitely had the heart necessary to make the strategies I had used work for her. And she did!

Who knew this stack of stuff would eventually lead to a massive movement to change the field of senior centered real estate!

As I was running through the airport one day I got a call from Michele. She was telling me about another agent who had inquired with her about working with the mature market. Michele told me that I should put together a class and start training agents on how to create a successful senior real estate specialty. By this time, Michele was doing quite well with her own practice, and I told her that she should do it. I was exhausted from travel and frankly, making a substantial income in my current role. We agreed this would be something to revisit "later."

Fast forward...

Nothing lasts forever and that you can count on. Traveling had gotten the best of me and I was finding that I had lost the passion for BOLD. My kids were in their final years of high school and I missed my husband and friends (the few I still had left). It was time for a change.

Much like back in Chapter 1, the maintenance phase of the adventure had shown up and I was ready for something new to tackle. I just wasn't sure what it would be. I was once again searching.

Sawdust

One day my business coach and friend, Mark, shared with me a metaphor about sawdust. He said, "Nikki, when you are developing, constructing and building, you are creating a lot of sawdust. Yes, you have the creation (whatever it might be), but on the floor all around you is the sawdust you have generated. Most people just turn it into compost or simply leave it behind. You have the unique ability to see it as something of value. You sweep it up, repurpose it, and turn it into yet another creation - one that adds value to others."

He was right!

During the five years we were designing, growing, and running our senior centered real estate and move management teams, we generated a lot of sawdust. Unfortunately, a lot of the actual tangible sawdust had been sold with our original business. Fortunately, what I couldn't put my hands on was stored neatly away in the archives of my brain.

Time to sweep up some sawdust and turn it into something useful. Yes, I realize we have shifted from pasta to sawdust - just roll with it.

The first official educational course I wrote we titled Success in Seniors Real Estate. It resulted from a culmination of factors. First, Michele poking and prodding me to take my stack of materials and the coaching I had given her to create a formal curriculum for real estate agents on how to create a successful senior-focused niche. Second, the desire to start a new project - one of my own making and one that was designed for a more relational agent. Lastly, a passion for helping a larger number of downsizing seniors. I knew this would require leverage - significantly more agents doing what we originally did in our home market of Oklahoma City.

Seniors Real Estate Institute was born.

With wide acceptance of Success in Seniors Real Estate as a course, we were encouraged by graduates to formalize our program and create a community where like-minded people could gather. The Seniors Real Estate Institute was then founded, followed by the Certified Senior Housing Professional (CSHP) designation.

My passion as a coach, trainer, speaker, and educator was reignited. I was able to take my formal education and anecdotal experience, along with Chris's talent for operations and logistics, and combine them together into an organization with a mission to educate, equip, and empower real estate sales professionals to better serve seniors all around the world.

Learn more about serving seniors as a real estate professional at seniorsrealestateinstitute.com.

CHAPTER 7: STARTING OVER

CREATING MORE SAWDUST

The Seniors Real Estate Institute was just beginning to take off and we were enjoying life in Austin (with a new grand baby nearby) when we got a call from my brother informing us that my dad wasn't well. It only took one trip back home to recognize that I couldn't be the daughter I wanted to be and provide the support necessary from seven hours away.

You may recall from previous chapters that I never intended to move back to Oklahoma. Not only were we enjoying milder winters in southern cities, but by this point we had all but relinquished our professional ties to Oklahoma. We hadn't renewed our respective real estate licenses and I had let my license as a professional counselor lapse as well. Why keep them up if we weren't ever planning to live in Oklahoma again. Right? Famous last words.

Despite having been gone for nearly a decade, our reputations as senior real estate experts remained. In fact, it wasn't long after returning "home" when people began reaching out and inquiring about our newest adventure. Most were surprised we were back and more than a little curious as to why! "We're coaching and training real estate agents around the country who serve the mature market," I would say when asked. Then people began to ask us for local support and advice about real estate and senior living issues.

You may be wondering what happened to the agents who bought our original business just seven years prior. Well, much to my disappointment, they dissolved the senior division of the business as the market began to shift during the real estate bust and recession around 2008-2012. They began focusing more toward online leads and distressed properties - for what reason I don't know. As it turns out, this decision became their loss and our eventual gain.

Never say never.

I began to wonder if this was a sign. Did this nearly decade-long journey around the country lead us back here for some crazy purpose? Was it to relaunch our real estate practice? Surely not, I thought.

Despite the fact I held active real estate licenses in Florida, Texas, and Louisiana, these would do me little good in Oklahoma. Having let my Oklahoma real estate license lapse was beginning to feel like an epic mistake. Going back into the real estate sales business would require additional expense and effort I had not contemplated.

Unlike the first time I entered the real estate industry at age 21, this time I had the benefit of past experience. Launching again didn't feel nearly as overwhelming. And when we started our first specialty practice over 15 years ago, we had no gauge for knowing how long it would take nor any models to follow. This time we could draw on our previous experience and establish benchmarks based on earlier successes.

Having established both a highly profitable and rewarding business in only five years once before, I knew we could do it again.

As we geared up to relaunch our senior-centered real estate team, I didn't want to make any assumptions. A lot can change in only a short time and I had been out of both aging services and sales for a while. To refamiliarize myself with local issues, I once again conducted focus groups, talked to as many people as I could, and attended networking events. These efforts helped me get current about local senior living related issues and assemble a highly qualified resource team.

I also went to work cataloguing the area's retirement communities (including the new ones built since our departure), taking community tours, and creating relationships with key industry connectors. Naturally, we didn't yet have strong referral relationships with independent, assisted, and longterm care communities like we had before - that would take more time.

Older, wiser, and better informed about the current

evolution of the senior living industry, I made an executive decision. Rather than attempting to partner with all the senior living communities in our area, we would only partner only with those who shared our values of service, education, and empowerment. We would focus on quality over quantity. A lesson I had learned the hard way years before.

Consumer education and empowerment.

Education is still (and always will be) a key component in helping people make informed decisions about when, where, and how to downsize or move. When people are uncertain, confused, or overwhelmed, they stay put. It's not that they don't want or need to move, but they are simply scared or ill-equipped to take action.

We could have attempted to partner with communities (like we did previously) to offer education, but we decided to go direct to the consumer this time. Yes, it required a larger initial investment on our part, but I knew the reward would outweigh the risk in the end. By being the organizer of the events, we controlled the message, guaranteeing that seminars were truly educational and not just another sales pitch. We also controlled the marketing message and the size and makeup of the events.

Our first seminar attracted 45 eager and attentive seniors. Not bad for a January event in Oklahoma on the topic of reverse mortgages, but still not what I would consider a stellar turnout. The second seminar, however, packed the house. The capacity at our venue, a nearby public library, was 80 people (my goal number). When the doors opened at 10am I was informed that we were at 102 people. The room was full and several people were standing in line outside the door begging to come in. They told our team they would simply use their walker as seats - no problem. Unfortunately, it was a problem for the fire marshal. We had to turn people away. But what a nice problem to have!

At the time of this writing we are in the sixth year of offering regular monthly seminars. The series has its own brand, sponsors, and even a number of self-proclaimed "groupies." Attendance has grown to 175-200 attendees each month on average and we've begun offering a virtual option for those who can't make it in person. We hosted two seminars a month for over a year at one point to accommodate the growing numbers. That was exhausting. We went back to only one per month after that.

During the pandemic in 2020, we found an online solution so people could attend safely from home. Naysayers told us that seniors wouldn't participate in online education, but we found that with a little encouragement and the occasional tech support, our audiences continued to show up in record numbers. They are already beginning to fill the rooms again.

To learn more about how to host educational seminars geared toward downsizing senior audiences, visit www.ultimateseniorseminarsolution.com.

One of the many things we have learned as a result of offering public talks and seminars over the years is that we aren't as reliant on senior living communities for referrals like we were in the beginning. I love our community partners, and many of them refer to us regularly. It's important to me, however, to ensure people make informed choices about where they move. By being the first point of contact (or at least earlier in the process) we can provide education and support. This way they know their options and have the tools for better evaluating them. It also solidifies our value and better demonstrates our point of difference as real estate professionals.

Branding

Much debate went into how we would brand ourselves as we launched the second time around. With our former tagline no longer ours to use, we had to decide how we wanted to be known. Did we want to go "all in" as experts in the mature market, or did we want to generalize and make our senior speciality a sub-category or side-gig?

Reflecting on our greater mission to create a community of real estate professionals serving seniors all around the globe, it was decided that we would indeed go "all in" branding our team as mature market experts. OKC Mature Moves Real Estate Services was formed. We knew it could be a risk, but we wanted to see how the market would respond.

The market embraced our brand.

In only two short years after launching, we were

closing nearly 50 transactions annually - virtually all of them involving longtime homeowners or those downsizing from larger homes to smaller ones. We had proven (for the second time) a senior centered niche could be a valid and replicable real estate business model.

We later changed the name of our real estate team to Buckelew Realty Group, but didn't change anything else as it related to our real estate marketing strategy or branding. OKC Mature Moves became the name of our senior move management business, catering to Buckelew Realty Group clients exclusively (at first). Both Buckelew Realty Group and OKC Mature Moves serve as primary sponsors of our now highly visible seminar series, along with other vendor partners and senior communities who share our passion for education.

Growth and Expansion: Take Two

We were in our 20's and 30's when building our first real estate team. Selling five to six homes each month without the support of an extended team was manageable. Our hiring intentions were also different back then. At that point we fully expected to be working in the day-to-day operations for a period of several years (or decades). Now, moving into our 50's we are looking forward to more travel days and fewer work days.

The new goal: Replace myself sooner than later.

Being a listing focused business (80% listings and 20% buyers), we fully recognized that we might be leaving business on the table by choosing not to heavily pursue buyers. Having previously employed two to three buyer agents at any given time, however, we also knew the kind of oversight and management this requires. Leads for buyers, now driven largely by the internet, are more challenging to convert and require much more effort than ever before. Being in the midst of a strong seller's market doesn't help matters.

So, while the industry gurus strongly emphasize the buyer agent model, we opted for the path less traveled -- a strong and multi-talented listing specialist first.

With over three decades of real estate experience under our belts, Chris and I have coached, trained, and recruited hundreds (maybe thousands) of sales people. Finding those who are talented in sales and customer service, but who also have empathy and concern for others is rare. There are plenty of agents with excellent sales skills, but who lack empathy. There are also many with huge hearts, but who can't seem to close a sale.

I knew I had found a unicorn when I met the agent who would later become our listing manager. To be fair, this was our third stab in three years at hiring for this position. Each time we learned both what we needed and what we didn't need in our future team members.

Lots of spaghetti.

Lots of sawdust.

Shannon possessed a rare combination of skill and heart, with the added bonus of being able to juggle lots of balls in the air simultaneously. Having had a decade or more of retail management and customer service experience prior to real estate, she recognizes the need to be strategic in approaching both people and transactions. What she lacks in patience, she makes up for in her communication technique and sincere concern for others.

I had originally met Shannon when she attended our training program for becoming a Certified Senior Housing Professional. Three years later, she was succeeding in her own business when I approached her about coming to work with our team. I knew I needed someone who was capable of managing the many details of multiple transactions, but who also shared our moral and ethical values. We struck a deal that would be a win-win for all of us.

Another run at move management

As I said earlier, move management has been the key component of our overall value proposition in serving downsizing homeowners. Unlike our first attempt at specialization, a time when move managers were scarce and the industry was brand new, there are more options now. That said, there are advantages to keeping this role in-house versus outsourcing to other providers.

By having our own move management company, we are able to ensure availability, control costs, and guarantee a level of quality unmatched by our competitors. The move managers I have encountered tend to be more transactional. They may handle the "stuff" and the logistics well, but they likely pay little (if any) attention to the emotional and psychological issues with which so many downsizing mature adults grapple.

We prefer a more relational approach. By taking the time to help people work through any phase of life tasks they may be facing, we not only serve as move managers who facilitate getting them and their stuff from point A to point B, but we also serve as legacy coaches. We help them grieve, heal, and reconcile the issues they may be dealing with as they make what is often a major life change. The biggest advantage to having both real estate and move management companies, however, is that it simplifies everything for the consumer. One stop shop. Turn-key operation. Soup to nuts.

Embracing change

The hardest part of owning a business for me has always been staffing and leadership. Specifically, losing team members and having to replace them. I realize this is just the nature of things, but nonetheless, I struggle with it. To date, we have had three move managers, and even as I write this, we are interviewing for the fourth. Let's be honest - it's not an easy job. It's physical, it's emotional (if we're doing it right), and it's fast-paced. There are multiple moving parts and the stakes are high. It's certainly not for the faint of heart.

Each time we change move managers, I become one in the interim. I actually enjoy the job and if I thought our organization could grow to its fullest potential by my being the senior move manager, I would do it. Chris will tell you, however, it's not my zone of genius. So, the hunt continues and this won't likely be the last.

Nurturing Relationships

After hiring and keeping great team members, the most difficult task in our business is staying in touch. This is especially true for two primary reasons: 1) We engage a significant number of people through speaking events who are still in the early stages of the sales cycle, and 2) Relationship-centered prospecting takes more time and more personalization than transactional prospecting.

Not everyone who comes to our monthly events is ready to sign a listing contract. Our goal and our promise to them is to stay in touch and be a resource until such time they are ready to make a change. It's not just prospecting for us, however, it's truly our intention to be a resource to them whether they move or not. If they are dealing with home repairs, a need for in-home care, legal, or financial issues, we are committed to connecting them with reputable local vendors and resources.

It's the right thing to do.

That's where Naomi comes in. Five years ago (give or take) Naomi's title started as inside sales assistant and then virtual assistant. Her first job description was to follow up with seminar attendees by phone, finding out what they thought of the seminar and what we could do to help them further. She also called them every month to remind them of the next event.

This isn't a job for just anyone. Naomi is special. She loves our people and she goes the extra mile to show it. Most of our seminar attendees and clients have no idea she isn't local. They frequently ask when they get to meet her in person. Working from several states away, Naomi's title is now Executive Assistant. As an invaluable full time team member, I'm not joking when I say she manages and/or coordinates virtually everything involved in my professional life and much of my personal world as well. And no, you can't hire her.

Oh my how things have changed!

One aspect of doing business that has changed significantly in the past two decades is the shift from paper to digital. Not only has the internet become the source of information for most people, email has replaced mail, and digital signatures have become the norm in virtually all industries.

Not in our world...

Yes, we use email. Yes, we use the internet. And yes, we certainly enjoy it when we have a client who can sign digitally from time to time. The reality, however, is that many of our clients, albeit computer literate, prefer the pen and paper method. More than the comfort of good ol' handwritten signatures, however, I think it's more about meeting with us toe to toe and eye to eye that matters.

Trust comes with being in person.

Beyond contracts, we also use the postal service for much of our marketing and other correspondence. We print and mail a monthly article with a cover letter on our letterhead, as well as quarterly invitations which include our printed seminar schedule. All of these things could be emailed, but many of our clients - even those with email addresses - only check their email occasionally. They are also inundated by junk mail, scams, and advertisements, so getting something in the mail is special. It means it's important. It means they are important.

Envisioning what's next.

It's hard to say what the next chapter will look like for our teams and our businesses. As much as I would love to say that we have one, three, and five year plans that are outlined with precision and which I fully expect to play out exactly as written, that wouldn't be true. I know that's contrary to what all the goal setting experts teach, but then I'm not a goal setting expert. I am an entrepreneur and a visionary who has found residential real estate sales to be my vehicle for serving others. Nothing more and nothing less.

If I had to guess, I suspect that our real estate team will close somewhere around eighty or more sales this calendar year. Somewhere around 60% of those clients will employ our move management team. Not bad considering the status of the pandemic remains a mystery. I also suspect we will have at least two more full time team members who will join us in our mission to serve longtime homeowners and downsizing mature adults. There is little doubt that our brands will become even more recognized in the marketplace as in-person seminars resume following the pandemic.

Beyond that, I simply have faith that we will continue to positively impact the lives of the clients we serve.

However many. However few.

CHAPTER 8: LIVING MY LEGACY

JOINING WITH OTHERS ALONG THE PATH

As I said in the introduction, this book wasn't intended to be a guide or manual for those seeking to create a real estate practice focused on serving seniors. It's simply my story. And if you've read this far, there must be something about the path I followed that resonated with you. Maybe you saw, heard, or experienced yourself somewhere in these pages.

Or it's possible that you are in the place where I was? Searching for something different? Searching for meaning and purpose in your chosen vocation? Maybe you're curious about how to combine your vocation with your passion for service.

Allow me to share with you a few final thoughts as

you continue along on your journey. Whether you are already serving seniors in your current real estate practice, or are just beginning to contemplate doing so, I would like to encourage you. Lord knows I've needed a lot of encouragement myself (and still do from time to time).

In the course materials for Success in Seniors Real Estate, we share seven fundamentals for creating a successful senior real estate niche. These principles are based on my own experience and those of others who have followed a similar path.

Start here, and if you are truly being called to this role in life, the rest will most certainly fall into place over time. I'm living proof of that to be sure.

---

7 Fundamentals for Successfully Serving Seniors

Be all about seniors. Commit to understanding the unique and often complex issues related to aging, family systems, late-life moves, and the goals and expectations of long-time homeowners. Read. Ask questions. Get curious.

Become an expert advisor. Serve as a fiduciary when assisting mature homebuyers and sellers by being knowledgeable about local resources and the many senior housing options available. Get outside the real estate bubble.

Be a reliable and resourceful project manager.

Serve as the hub of the transaction, leveraging the necessary resources and implementing relevant relocation solutions. This type of lifestyle change is more complex than a simple real estate deal.

Be enjoyable to work with. When dealing with clients, trusted advisors, vendors, and colleagues, be communicative, engaged, pleasant, empathetic, and professional - always. The world can be a kinder place if we work at it.

Share your passion. Find joy in your work each day and recognize it as a way of serving or ministering to others. You can make a nice living while also making a positive difference.

Become highly competent and skilled. Focus on self-mastery and gain expertise in negotiating contracts, pricing and marketing homes, problem solving, and communicating effectively. Don't settle for average.

Be relationship-centered. Put people ahead of profits, value others, and appreciate the human connection inherent in all business relationships. People matter.

Full circle

When asked as a young person what I wanted to be when I grew up, I had several aspirations. None of them included real estate sales or serving seniors. I wanted to be a lawyer, a teacher, a preacher, a country music singer, and an investigative reporter. Today, I find myself getting to do all the things that I found most interesting about these professions.

I get to advise people and guide them through complex processes and transactions regularly, yet I spend most of my days educating, equipping, and encouraging. Whether I am front and center speaking at one of our seminars or events, or I am alone in the living room with a grieving family, I am ministering. I love the applause and appreciation that follows the delivery of a powerful educational seminar (and I get to use a microphone). And lastly, as an advocate for the most vulnerable of our elders, I get to be a truth teller, helping people avoid pitfalls and find solutions to problems associated with getting older.

I am often reminded of what Art once said, "It's all coming together nicely."

Now it's your turn.

Whether you are currently selling real estate or find yourself curious about whether it could be the right path for you, just remember that life is full of twists, turns, hills, and valleys. Nothing moves forward in a straight line.

Each of us has the potential to change lives for the better. You can, will, and do make a difference!

Taking the first step is the key.

APPENDIX

10 Myths and Truths about Specialization

Having worked as a mature market expert for two decades and logging thousands of coaching hours with new and seasoned real estate sales professionals, I have found that what holds people back isn't their abilities, motivation, or even skill. What holds us back is our mindset.

Each one of us has limiting beliefs. Some have more than others. So to truly experience success, we must first identify the beliefs which are limiting progress and replace them with new ones - ones that serve our current needs, desires, and goals.

Myth #1: I'm not smart enough.

I start with this misconception for two reasons. First of all, it was the biggest of my own limiting beliefs. You might have made note that I have a number of degrees and initials after my name. That is because I have lived most of my life thinking that I just wasn't smart enough. The fact is, I have always been smart enough and so are you. So, is it okay to strive for more knowledge through education? Yes, of course it is! Just take a moment to acknowledge WHY you are doing it.

The truth is, there are far more people having gone through our training programs succeeding in the mature market without college degrees than there are people with them. If you have a college education and degrees hanging on your wall then use them to your advantage. If you don't, let go of any misconception that you somehow "need" them to achieve your goals in this business.

Myth #2: I don't know enough.

Good news, there are a number of solutions to this dilemma. The truth is that no one knows all they need to know when embarking upon a new adventure. You didn't know how to drive when you first learned to drive. You didn't know how to explain a listing or sales contract when you first got your real estate license either. But you learned. This time is no different than those times. You will find mentors, guides, books, classes and other resources. Then you take your foot off the brake and apply it to the accelerator. In the beginning you will take it slow, but in no time you will be drinking coffee, reading a text, putting on makeup, and talking to Siri (you know you do it) all while safely navigating to your destination. Learn what you need to learn over time and just keep rolling.

Myth #3: I know everything I need to know.

This common misconception may be worse than feeling like you don't know enough. The truth is that those who have taken a weekend course to get their senior real estate designation often approach the mature market with a mistaken sense of superiority and false confidence. Somehow the National Association of REALTORS short course has been deemed as the gold standard for senior real estate education. I can't tell you how many people (a lot) have said to me over the years that the SRES course, while helpful, left them with more questions than answers. There is always more to learn - always!

I know this first hand because it was the first course I took back in 2002. I later taught a couple of their courses and was involved in a committee tasked with rewriting some of the content (they revised it very little after 10+ years). The reality is that any class is a great starting off point, but it's not the end all be all solution to better serving seniors longterm (or becoming the best you can be). Keep learning, keep studying, keep growing! The world is evolving and we must continue to adapt.

Myth #4: I'm too young to work with seniors.

If you're reading this book and you're in your 20's, 30s, or even 40's you may wonder what qualifies you to deal with the issues associated with aging. The good news is that you have a model to follow. I was only 27 and my husband was 24 when we started specializing in helping seniors. There will always be a few skeptics out there who may question your abilities, but when you are armed with knowledge, along with a vocabulary to convey that knowledge, your age becomes a non-issue. The truth...being successful is never about age.

Myth #5: I'm a senior myself so...

"Since I'm a senior myself, I figured it only made sense to specialize in the senior market." If I've heard this once, I've heard it a hundred times (as my dad used to say). Let me be brutally honest here. Age really has nothing to do with whether or not you should or shouldn't specialize in the mature market. Being a senior yourself is not a prerequisite for specialization and in no way predicts whether or not you will be effective as a mature market expert. I think what I love most about having "seniors" participate in our courses (under the pretense of serving their peers) is that they find at least as much value personally from the material as they do professionally.

Myth #6: Everyone who specializes in the 55+ market cares about seniors.

When we field calls from people about taking SREI courses, we always inquire about their motivation. Sometimes we get answers that go something like this. "There are so many seniors out there and this market is only going to get bigger. It just makes sense to learn how to market to them so I can gain more market share in my area." While this sentiment may seem fairly innocuous on its surface, it makes the hair on the back of my neck stand up.

For some, specializing in seniors really means creating another profit center by getting good at exploiting seniors. Listen to your inner voice - you'll know the difference.

Myth #7: Serving seniors will be easy.

With over 10,000 baby boomers turning 65 every second, one might think that specializing in the mature market is the equivalent of fishing in a barrel, right? Think again. While there is no question concerning the opportunity before us, there is little about this particular specialty (or selling real estate as a career for that matter) that's easy.

I feel it's especially important to mention this for the newer people in the field. As you create your goals, I encourage you to think big and aim high. I also want you to plan longterm. If you are building a business rather than simply shooting for a few sales here and there, you will want to establish models, systems, and processes so that you can scale your business over time.

Certainly some of what you will do in your business will feel easy. These are the things that are likely natural to you - your zone of genius. Other parts of the business will be "hard" or more challenging. Embrace all of it. Stay the course - even when the going gets tough.

Myth # 8: Specializing in seniors means losing non-senior business.

Not only did our sales volume increase when we

began to specialize, both our senior-centered units and our non-senior units increased. It didn't hurt our business - it propelled it. This could be attributed to passion for the business again, an improved marketing strategy, or dumb luck. We try not to overthink it - we just enjoy what we do and keep doing it!

Myth #9: Certifications and designations are necessary to be successful.

Growing any business is a grand experiment and having a strong foundation and model to follow can certainly shorten the learning curve. That said, nothing can take the place of taking action, failing, and then taking action again -- over and over and over. Certifications and designations are simply letters behind your name. Nothing more and nothing less.

In the beginning years after founding Seniors Real Estate Institute and offering the foundational course, Success in Senior Real Estate, we were encouraged by graduates to create a certification. I was actually against it. They would say, "We worked so hard..." and then ask, "Don't we get some sort of recognition?" The fact is, no certification or designation is the magic pill to success.

The only reason I eventually caved and decided to create the Certified Senior Housing Professional (CSHP) was so agents could more easily identify other graduates around the country, making it easier to connect clients to the best agents in the business.

Clients aren't looking for letters after your name, they

are looking for you to be the expert - the authority. This comes through quality education and dedicated time on task over time.

Myth #10: My market is saturated with agents specializing in seniors.

Don't be confused by agents who say they specialize and those who actually do. Few agents, even those with designations, actually dive into the deep end to fully engage seniors in a meaningful and helpful way. Most are simply marketing to seniors - not specializing. What they mean by specializing is that they have learned how to market to them - not serve them.

If you will go the extra mile to truly learn about your clients and how to better serve their needs, I can promise that your true competition will be few and far between!

CCRC - Continuing Care
- offer levels of care - move
w/in facility based on need

Independent living - 55+ or 62+
communities - services
transportation, meals, cleaning
call buttons, activities
Assisted Living - need ADL help
Aging in Place
Intergenerational Housing

Active Adult Retirement Comm.

Nursing Care - smaller facility
Nursing Home - Large scale care facility

Involvement in housing decision =
more/less satisfaction w/ move

LET'S CONNECT

Connect with Nikki on LinkedIn
https://www.linkedin.com/in/coachnikki

Connect with SREI on LinkedIn
https://www.linkedin.com/company/seniorsrealestateinstitute

Connect with SREI on Facebook
https://www.facebook.com/SeniorsRealEstateInstitute

Connect with Nikki and SREI on Instagram
https://www.instagram.com/nikkibuckelew

SREI Resources and Classes

Seniors Real Estate Institute
http://www.seniorsrealestateinstitute.com

Success in Seniors Real Estate - 3 part class (optional certification)
http://www.successinseniorsrealestate.com

Ultimate Senior Living Seminar Solution
https://seniorsrealestateinstitute.com/ultimate-senior-living-seminar-solution

Managing Mature Moves
https://seniorsrealestateinstitute.com/managing-mature-moves

Downsizing Made Easy Presentation System
https://seniorsrealestateinstitute.com/downsizing-made-easy-presentation-system

OKC-Based Relocation Resources

Buckelew Realty Group - Oklahoma City, OK
http://www.buckelewrealtygroup.com

OKC Mature Moves - Professional Move Management - Oklahoma City, OK
http://www.okcmaturemoves.com

Senior Living Truth Series - Oklahoma City and beyond
http://www.seniorlivingtruthseries.com

Recommended Reading

Buckelew, Nikki (2018). Residential Reasoning in Older Adult Married Dyads: A Phenomenological Study (https://tinyurl.com/BuckelewDissertation)

Golant, Stephen (2015). Aging in the Right Place.

Keller, G., Jenks, J., Papasan, J. (2003). The Millionaire Real Estate Agent.

LaPorte, Danielle (2014). Firestarter Sessions. A Soulful + Practical Guide to Creating Success on Your Own Terms.

Solie, David (2004). How to Say It to Seniors: Closing the Communication Gap with Our Elders.

ABOUT THE AUTHOR

Nikki Buckelew is a downsizing coach, trainer, and author. She has authored books focused on late life relocations including *Downsizing Made Easy: 5 Easy Steps to a Successful Move* and *Moving Mom and Dad: 5 Mistakes Adult Children of Aging Parents Make and How to Avoid Them.*

She and her husband founded the Seniors Real Estate Institute, a coaching and training organization with a mission to equip real estate professionals to better serve mature clients.

Informing her work are over two decades of experience helping families through the downsizing process as the owner of residential real estate brokerages and move management companies, anecdotal stories and best practices of those having studied under her, countless focus groups and academic research, and years of educational experience including degrees in gerontology and psychology.

Buckelew is known for her candid but caring presentation style, not holding anything back when it comes to approaching tough topics. Her work has served to help thousands of mature homeowners navigate the complexities of late-life relocations.

When she is not writing, teaching, or coaching, she is spending time with her grandchildren or enjoying time on a boat (preferably where the water is salty and blue).

Made in the USA
Monee, IL
16 August 2021